Against the Meanwhile
3 Elegies

Other books by Mark Irwin

Umbrellas in the Snow, 1985

The Halo of Desire, 1987

Translations

Notebook of Shadows
Selected Poems of Philippe Denis, 1982

Ask the Circle to Forgive You
Selected Poems of Nichita Stănescu, 1964–1979
trans. with Mariana Carpinisan, 1983

Mark Irwin

Against
the Meanwhile

3 Elegies

 Wesleyan University Press
Middletown, Connecticut

for Peter Salm, Walter Strauss, Robert Wallace
for my mother and father

for Venetia

Copyright © 1988 by Mark Irwin

"The Wisdom of the Body" Sections 1,3,4,6,7, and 9 and
"Against the Meanwhile" originally appeared in *The Kenyon Review*.

I would like to thank Philip Church, John Drury, and John Hobbs for
editorial suggestions, and I would like to thank Gregory Kharas for in-
spiration and friendship.

All inquiries and permissions requests should be addressed to the
Publisher, Wesleyan University Press, 110 Mt. Vernon Street, Mid-
dletown, Connecticut 06457

LIBRARY OF CONGRESS CATALOGING-IN-PUBLICATION DATA
Irwin, Mark.
    Against the meanwhile : 3 elegies / Mark Irwin.
        p. cm.
    ISBN 0-8195-2150-7   ISBN 0-8195-1151-X (pbk.)
    1. Elegiac poetry, American.   I. Title.
PS3559.R95A7   1988
811'.54—dc19   87-27244 CIP

Manufactured in the United States of America

FIRST EDITION

Wesleyan Poetry

Contents

I

The Wisdom of the Body

Once, everything only once. Once and no more. And we too,
once. Never again. But to have been
this once. . . .

—RILKE, *The Duino Elegies*

The Wisdom of the Body

1

April. The day is all middle.
The center diminished to everywhere.
The listening soil in light of all else.

I carry the trout to the garden,
lay them on the wooden table.

An hour ago
their gills were hearts of color
flashing like tulips from the water.
Now their mouths open and close on no

water, this slower knife.

My thumbs pray on the split middle,
scraping away the floral waste
as the body quakes in a final arch—
everything inside going out.

These still bright organs
belong in the earth to grow dull
quick under the tickling legs of flies and ants—
their telling stench
like the female scent to the male.

2

How the body goes on talking.
You make pots and vases.
You tuck and knead the clay.
Your lovely hands rub the woman into the work
you glaze and fire.

Behind your studio is another kiln, larger,
faster to end with less,
the fetid odor of burning flesh:
corpses of the poor.

The attendants do little.
Polishing their cars, they wait for bodies.
How much can one grow accustomed to?

The body dressed in flames will slightly rise
as if to sit.

3

Light is what lacks in each of us.
The body is drawn toward light.

Hundreds of ants
line the walk to the garden.
They steer in perfect files,
an unswerving syntax between tiny monuments.
The sun is their compass.

If placed in an open tube
with food at one end,
the larva of the browntail moth
will crawl toward the light
and die of starvation.
The halo of desire.

4

I weed and turn the garden.
Everywhere there are worms
sliding through the rings of themselves.
All touch, they love the dark.

I hoe the soil fine as sand
then plant mustard seeds.
Small things become each other,
each grain with the hill of the ant.
Their houses are little clocks

and they too have gardens,
underground chambers
where bits of fruit mixed with excrement
form tiny acres of bacteria.
They feed off cultures that go on and on.

Spinach, peas, lettuce—
Then last, tomatoes and pumpkins.
In dusk-light the soil looks blue,
then goes slate

                    deep as water
as the stars appear.

5

Summer morning, the day before the solstice.
The trees are gauzed with light.
It is the time of domes and steeples,
and blond-headed children running home late.

I remember six months back:
the small day at five o'clock
like a piece of coal on fire,
a halo of tangerine on black.
The year seen through a camera;
this the final image of that.

Lettuce and spinach unfold in the mist.
The garden's a tent of oxygen,
the earth a world of insects.

The lacewing's body is the color of lettuce.
Green, faint as the beginning of any seedling.
Almost transparent.
I can almost see through the body.

6

Termites have taken over the stump.
Near the base, beneath the rotted bark,
a kingdom of larvae.
Snow-white eggs in the silken dirt.

How the large one, having lost a wing,
drags itself away—
perhaps to shed the other?

Is she a queen?
For the nuptial pair have wings
they lose after mating,
as if to say—
Flight is required,
conception an airy thing.

For the bird and insect,
wings are organs.
Flight a conceiving of space.
The bird a perfect center.

7

The languor of this longest of evenings.
What used to be called *Mid-Summer Night's Eve.*
How mistletoe was held to be sacred
seen in the sun's fire
at the two turning points of the year.
If picked at midnight
and thrown into the air,
the place where it landed would reveal the earth
in a blue flame.

In December
when the oak is bare,
its green leaves are an April,
its berries white as tubers.

There are times when the world reveals itself.
We look through our lives,
or perhaps the earth is looking through us.

8

Tonight as you
draw your knees to your chest,
I remember another inseparable space,
feel its close pulse

as now your body curves
to question,
and then by questioning
answer mine.

The wisdom of the body.

And so you sleep and I get up
and walk to the porch
where all night a moth taps the bulb.

Mistletoe, I think,
and how two doves led Aeneas
through a woods to find it.
The trick he used to catch the ferryman
and ride the river Styx to hell.
How deep that bark
sank with his living weight.

9

Today is October.
Except for the pumpkins everything is spent—
the last fruits of the sun's fire.
On one dead, already dry vine,
a cocoon's swollen pustule.
I separate the dry pod from the stem,
then split it with my thumb to find
a thick and formless jell—

the caterpillar gone,
dissolved to a fetal pool of white.
Its center diminished to everywhere.

We too once moved in a sleep like nothing
when liquids giving form
spelled out time's possibility.
So too when put in the earth
the body gives up shape.

10

The afternoon's a theater of orange,
each dry sound
a shade of darker growing color:
the ochre snap of weeds, the faint tock of dropping leaves.

Three o'clock in the afternoon
when for a moment the day pauses
with the weight of itself.

A schoolbus groans and brakes to a stop.
The children are returning to their imaginary worlds.
I hear their laughter through the window,
I feel its color through the glass.

Bees doze on the sill,
feeding on the warmth of the house.
They are their own last flower.
Their target bodies never miss.

11

Evening and everything is falling.
The sun is the weighted end of a wheel
and the trees are gears crumbling away in color.
No longer a movement

they stand like wooden fixtures,
monuments to space unfolding
as the stars begin to appear

and you stare at the paling sky
and weigh

nothing.

II

Against the Meanwhile

So then I found in all things good and
evil, love and wrath, in creatures of
reason as well as in wood, in stone, in
earth, in the elements, in men and ani-
mals. Withal, I considered the little spark
"man" and what it might be esteemed to
be by God in comparison with this great
work of heaven and earth.

In consequence I grew very melancholy,
and what is written, though I knew it
well, could not console me.

—JAKOB BOEHME

Point Nine

1

Memory—hardly through the dusk
do the letters of that word break.
A boy calls his brother.
What the other boy walking home thinks
tossing the white ball up from the mitt—
                        then catching it,

the wandering present of the day's events
that in twenty years
will stray through the past
the way twilight strays toward the end of a street
then simply disappears
like the aggregate of shadow through leaves,
or the color of space beneath his bed.

            I will never forget
the first time I touched a leaf
etched in stone. The faint stir
like a wing through my spine. I
pressed it hard against my cheek
and hoped the mark would stay.
In half an hour it had vanished.

            Now, even the sand imprint
            blurs on that fossil.

Like history, we grow tired of things.
And they grow tired of us.

Near Pompeii, at the foot of Mount Vesuvius,
lies Herculaneum, the small village, now museum,
once buried in lava. A man and wife were found
embraced, caught in the soft stone.

As though love were the fossil of desire.

2

I stare at the zero ocean,
think of its vast decimaled floor.
How the sun eases through the surface

diffusing light with darkness
in this mildly shuttered room
where indistinguishable bands of blue
fade to violet.

        And as you descend further
what you believe to be lack of color,
what you believe to be black
is only the depth

           the perfection of violet
until within the eye
only the vague tint lingers
within the breathing gills of the iris.

And whether you travel up,
or whether you travel down into water
           you will learn
about space through the same shades of color—
blue both circle and center.

3

The sea is in us all.
Watch the face of the breathing sleeper.
The aspirant pull and reach of each breath
like the suck of the tide on pebbles.

The thawing snow above the tree line
feeds rivulet, brook, to stream.
And what the fetus draws from the yolk
moves to the heart, eyes, and limbs,
while capillaries fray through the lungs.

Point Eight

1

Cybele, I begin with you
who rose from the black stone
where nothing grows
and so became mother to all
in the endless cycle
of animal, mineral, and vegetal.

I do not know much about science,
but I know that nature
miniaturizes the world to possess it,
and that evolution is all.

Not the evolution of man,
bird, fish, insect, or plant—
but of the infinitely small
which moves toward something much larger
like the conflagration of a star
and the loss of mass

that streams toward us
when hydrogen nuclei
combine to form helium.

What we gain is called sunlight,
because when energy is degraded
atoms tend to move
toward more disorderly states.

2

Now I know why Dionysus
held council at night,
why he crowned women's heads with flowers
and poured wine into their silver cups
                    until morning

when Apollo,
with gold-filleted locks
streaming onto his shoulders, stood
envious, that from such chaos
came order.

3

Entropy is such a god,
what it has become for us.

At Oak Ridge, Tennessee,
neutrons are slowed
in a swimming-pool reactor,
their trace, a visible blue glow
like the blush of science
upon man.

And the heat,
the vaporizing white glow
over Hiroshima and Nagasaki
is not so unlike
the careless free verse of lightning

that forked through the sky
when naive Semele
wished her lover to appear
in all his glory

except that no one,
no one will sew us back up
in his thigh.

And the final Renaissance
of Science
will come like an April
when daffodils bow in the snow.

4

When the egg weds with the sperm,
the fertilized cell
cleaves once, twice longwise
then finally across
to separate the animal part
from the yolk it feeds upon.

The upper living part
feeding from below
goes on and on dividing
a thousand times
with no increase in size

until the blastula appears,
its hollow sphere with a thin roof
a smaller model of the world.

I think this inward movement
in which life begins
must be like that moment

       when a child
looks at trees from a distance
and the blue evening bends all about
to cup their greenness

     as he stands
dumb with their beauty.

Point Seven

1

April.
Now, now is the time.
Seeds that were dried in the sun
are put in the earth when the moon is new

for they are tiny planets
grown from the mouths of flowers
higher, higher, knocking in their pods
to become scattered, buried, frozen all winter.

But when the ground thaws, they will know.
When it rains, they will know,
drawing back up the moisture,

which is like remembering
after having forgotten, after having been dry,
after having been frozen,

until the sun warms like a kind pain
and something inside stirs.

Something whose first paling urge
issues both root and tendril
as the seed husk flays and the kernel splits
and the tiny green stem
lifts its pair of leaves toward sunlight

in a spiraling force that balances
the root's vertical thrust.

2

And the moon waxing,
the moon tugged out of the earth
will tug on the seed opening.

And if you see this
then you will know.

You will know to lie down
among the first green seedlings.
You will know to lie down and place
one stone in your mouth

and stare at the moon
bleach-white and shadow-pocked
until you feel its chalk-light in your skull,
until you taste the earth and your blood in that stone
and feel its tide move from your heart.

Seeds and moons and stars.

Then you will dig your hands into the dirt
up to the wrists, up to the elbows
until you feel the pulse of the earth.

3

And what is the earth
but a larger seed
that blooms

cerulean and green
beneath the Milky Way
spiraling, spiraling out
like the nebulaed thumbprint of gods.

4

I know little about religion
but I think men
should worship trees,

their huge canopied tops
dividing to branches, branches to twigs,
and twigs to capillaried leaves.

We all struggle toward sun
and what the lungs exchange
is not so unlike the breathing work of leaves.

I stand on the sawed-off stump
and with sap in my eyes
stare up through the flowering limbs.

Point Six

1

May, the first shirtless days—
my father's heavy foot on the spade
turning the earth he would hoe,
then rake, fine, fine as sand,

while I turned, eyes closed
under the sprinkler's rainbowed air,
catching water on my tongue.

Little boy, what are you doing,
he would always say.

Me, me, me. It was always me
who held the stakes, string, and seeds,
magic charms I would shake, rattle in their packets

then pour into his large, dirt-caked hands.
Why? why do they all look the same?

Point Five

1

Blind Heraclitus, who talked of fire
and sleep, said it.
The only reality

is change. What habit repels
to make life easy: our false
dream of continuity, the tropics of leisure

whose warmth dulls our sense of time.
Sunday morning after the party,
the little scuffs on the wooden floor,

record of joy and dancing
that in an hour will be waxed away.
Forgetting's gloss of memory.

2

Desire, too, is change.
I imagine a great fire
consuming abandoned tenements.
The hot wind blowing out windows
while among the bystanders who eagerly watch,

the arsonist himself
stands relieved
as flaming beams
collapse, wood
to ash.

3

Fear, too, is change
where the borders of desire
close, and all roads turn back
to the capital
of need.

Or hope. What at times
we abandon,
and accept for a moment
the present, whose promise lies
in that it offers none.

Point Four

1

In the beginning, when all collapsed
toward one center.

We are merely
a planet, speck of
that ongoing explosion
in which everything moves
outwardly. Galaxies equally receding,

centuries to them,
fireworks. Our lives, the held moment
when a roman candle
blossoms. Pompeii

to Hiroshima mere seconds, ephemera
of frozen color. Or on
a warm spring day
the viburnums' rush of pollen.

2

Like a dream fork
the tree of all species slowly
dividing, the one-celled protozoa
developing into slime mold
from which the first flat worm crawled?

And the tiny limbs
like hair gradually appeared.
Did the amoeba's breathing cilia
predict the legs of insects

while plants continued to bloom
from moss
to ferns and seed-bearing leaves?

Are bees not an answer to flowers?

3

Sometimes before sleep
or at some midpoint in the afternoon
when the sunlight falls watery through leaves,
my sight blurs into green
and I feel the presence of a body

all shoulders

struggling to hold
to the present
down whose steep bank it goes
slipping back forever.

4

Millions of years ago
when the rivers of South America dried up
and fish lay strewn on the banks
groping for water, only
the mutants
those with small gills
survived, burying themselves in silt,
breathing slowly
until the rains, the water might rise.
Thus a new species
the lungfish arose.

5

In the continual dawn by the sea
two men play chess.
The stakes are death. The game
hinges on a chain of mistakes
the winner will have made
all in his mind.
They sit in a rapturous
poise. The only consciousness is change,

and evolution
is a perpetuation of errors
that brings us toward
the consciousness of man.

Knowledge is movement,
the force that lacks us.
And we all live in the night.

6

The world goes on getting richer,
even in poverty
the detritus piles up:
bottles, cans, and worn-out
tires, the movement only partially stopped.

Perhaps salvation means
to die
just as one's goods entirely run out.
Bartleby faces the wall,
his last words
                "I would prefer not"

a wish to complete
his only remaining task
denied. The piety of such loss
like touching the face of God
or counting the bricks in that wall
to use what time is left.

7

Or why the accused
takes the executioner's knife
and twists it
into his own chest. A final leap
of humility
to simplify the task.

The saintly life of deprivation
whose common denominator is loss.

An old woman sits
staring into the future.
The uncashed check in her hand,
her son
dead. This is a wind
like time.

Point Three

1

This junkyard stretches for miles,
a cemetery of wrecked cars
some of which passed through red lights,
others hurtled off roads.

Hoods and fenders collapsed,
window glass shattered in accidents,
the perfect coincidence of time and space.

Hot rods groomed for high performance
and luxury sedans once handsomely chauffeured
now all move
at a standstill, ruled by
only the sun. Paint blisters,
thousands of hubcaps wink
and headlights doze in vacant stares.

Pokeweed and sumac grow wild
among the matted grass and jacked-up cars.
And like ants on something sweet,
men crawl about here looking for parts.

2

Over there an old Impala
its left rear door swung open
leans beside a tree.
A leg of ivy elegantly crawls
upon the mildewed carpet,
velour, and rotted foam of seats.

Nearby, two abandoned truck springs
spiral with trumpet and honeysuckle vine.
Cream and yellow blossoms
fountain among the junk,
while everywhere like common currency
wheel wells rust

into ochre and ferrous shades.
Miniature western landscapes,
perfect circles of sunlit flame.

I stare at a stripped-down engine block.
Each of the pistons, once
so perfectly timed, now
forever stopped
in a monument
to work.

Little teeth of rust like gears
continue to take it apart
as the long exchange begins,
machinery's slow grind
back into the earth.

3

I walk on and on through miles of debris
and look out over a hill, a horizon
filled with windshields.
To understand America
visit a junkyard in spring.

I step over drive shafts
strewn among wild parsnip and yarrow
where the bees, like tiny gold phantoms,
persist and continue to work.

Exhausted I turn and head toward the gate
and by the low evening sun
I begin to see
how each of our minds resembles
a junkyard of the past.
All that we wish had happened
cheated by time or place.

Before me, an old Chevy lies
surrounded by tall, cabbage-laced blossoms.
I rub my hand along its side,
sprinkle rust among the pollen,

knowing that tonight
as I lie at home in bed,
here the axle of stars will continue to turn,
turn above this place.

Point Two

I sit on the sand by the ocean
adding sticks to the fire
as the rain, infinitely gentle, begins
dousing away the flames,
petals growing back
into the flower's charred center
whose fruit would have been ash.

Now, I think about history
compared with the smaller endurance
of air, fire, water, earth;

the way time sanctifies memory
yet in desire both collapse.

If unable to remember
would there be any sense of time?
Or would we move about like ants
who only momentarily pause
touching muzzles over their dead?

To be human depends on reason
and on the capacity to desire.
But what can be figured out
when the mind is ruled by heart?

I think of the great explorers,
that still moment of discovery
reconciled with time.

Magellan gazing out over the Pacific,
forgetting what for.

Point One

1

Late in summer I come upon
the sudden image of rocks
in a streambed, dry, uttering my thoughts
that this must be like the awareness of pain
or the memory of growing old.

I even guess
what forgetting is like,
recall seeing that horse skull
socketed in earth

and the new grass
like the fine hair of an infant
taking hold
in the crumbling cage of the ribs.

I remember those orchards
where as children
we played hide-and-seek
beneath trees
whose fruits hung like pale lanterns, jewels

rising up
through a scent like sleep and tears,
a delicate balance
struggling like our breath to hold.

2

Now I walk toward Crown Hill
where we once gathered flowers;
and there, in the filtering shade of a maple,
a late dandelion, moonlike,
sways on its stem,
its opaque head a lens
that trembles to caress the light.

Held by its stalk in the sun
it is a child's wand
to touch with, or scepter
to plot a new constellation
of yellow stars.

Gently I blow
as though it were a candle
and I a man with too many birthdays
until the tiny head of seeds
explodes, spiraling up
in a cloud of silklike wings.

3

Faint, as when the wind
over a small pond
shifts, rippling the water's surface,

a song, that of an ice-cream truck,
floats out of the day
to hold in my mind,
filling it with a joy more distant.

And there, before me
where the blue sky bends over the earth
—children, shirtless, running.
Their tawny backs form a circled path

and their bodies groove the air
until it appears as if their turning arms
are the simple, continuous song
I have been hearing.

There was something behind the music,
something behind the skeletal braid
of those children on a hill,

the form apprehending all sensation
to which the patient flesh
held and felt all things.

III

Circling

. . . universally, relations stop nowhere,
and the exquisite problem of the artist is
eternally but to draw, by a geometry of
his own, the circle within which they
shall happily appear to do so . . .
      —HENRY JAMES,
        Preface to *Roderick Hudson*

February Ice

1

Facing the rain-streaked window
I watch the fire behind me
lick waking shapes,
shrunken, contained within each drop.

Father, when you and I watched waves
I thought of your letters,
your signature leveling out through years
to become the straight line
your father's was.

How long will this false spring last?

Among receding maps of snow
the tops of hills, their browns
and sickly greens show through—
a child's watercolors run together
on the warped, bumpy paper.

Pallid beneath a pewter sun
they seem a landscape of sadness,
a memory struggling to hold.

I light the room with tulips.
Their reds portray
another sadness

as they groove and sculpt the air,
and bleed such perfect oval petals.

How long will this false spring last?

2

Looking at your line-worn face
I finally understand the word
countenance. No more

the tight-set brow and pensive
lips when your temper flared
at jobs lost or money spent.

How your face upset
me as a child, and I wore
your each day's grimace

in my sleep. Is it not age
upon which emotions weigh?
The buoyed calm of a child's face

breaks to tears
at inconvenience,
but look at an old man's face—

the deep-cut brow and sagging
chin, the fat beneath the eyes
now add a graceful sorrow

while suffering and age dissolve
within the mild, haloed
light, we call humility.

3

And so it comes again, snow
gently undoing all boundaries.
Where the neighbor's farm

begins, definition
lessening, the exact math
of things exchanged

for a whim of gracious
contours. Now it strays,
roving over other snow

the way a stray thought roves,
sweeping, searching through
what light to find its source—

a memory, or imagination
growing? It keeps on
falling to

(like time's indifference)
diminish through accumulation.
Such outrageous drifts

are like desires,
wild finales spent
in a world

where lack of form
instills a fear—
making beauty more possible?

> *Still I can't forget*
> *the trail of dust*
> *that fell from my first grade*
>
> *wrist, as I ground*
> *the chalk down hard*
> *in embarrassment*
>
> *not knowing how*
> *to form each letter*
> *of the alphabet.*
>
> *That night, with big pencil*
> *and tears wetting*
> *the wide-ruled yellow*
>
> *paper, you taught me*
> *how to make them*
> *all, each one perfect.*

Each morning after that
with lunch pail and satchel
I arrived more confident

but always stared,
amazed, at the blackboard,
and wished that whoever

had washed it clean
could wash the fear
of error from my mind.

Even what tracks I've made
now have disappeared
in the white-masked air.

There, a rabbit
bounds like a heart
leaping from the chest of snow.

West, the first blue-
silvered tint breaks through
clouds swept so fast

it appears that light
were blowing toward
one dusk-lit hour of calm.

4

Toward the east
the huge snow cliffs stand
mantled in a rose
rounded like a woman's shoulders
about which the blue
wash of evening falls.

Turning, I walk back toward the house.
Now no wind moves. Pitch black
bears down from an imponderable height,
its enormous weight
eased by pinpricks of light.

The world shivers in primeval cold.
I follow my breath home.

5

All March we watch them grow
gainly, more beautiful
because vulnerable
like a child.

Slender beards of light
hang from the railing
inching lengthwise on dropper tips
pushing pear shapes
that silver
in a slight wind
before falling.

If music grew
it would be these in sunlight
falling.

6

For half an hour in zero weather
I stood by the window
afraid to enter.
I stood gazing at fire
through the elegant fire of ice

a cave of crystal
growing down
toward those flames, lithe, transparent-orange
fringed with blue, like a flower's
roving crown of petals.

Between the two I saw
my father's hand, a smaller flame
disappearing
like the woman's hand
that broke off icicles
and gave them to her son.

For half an hour in zero weather
I stood by the window afraid to enter.
I stood gazing at fire
through the jailed fire of ice.

7

Now as then the weather changed
all month, back and forth. Rag tag
days spitting flurries; or southern winds
and sun, brief, puzzling snow on lawns.

Days of give and take. Winter taking back
what spring gives: the songs
of birds increasing; birdsong a kind
of light, like that of March, growing louder.

Then as now I see other lights
that burn all day, strings
of lights.

        Mother, in my dream
you reach through sleep to take them,
a necklace of lights, jewels
set between
black hoods and chrome fenders.

With hands grown large through fever
you slip them off,
but the black parade
keeps moving.

I remember words like leaves
yellow now between us.
On ropes they set
the coffin in, the trunk of you
mahogany. There our stupid
faces pooled, oblong their agony
until the first clods struck hollow,
a knocking finally swallowed
in silken piles of earth,
followed by bouquets of flowers
that no one could arrange.

Above, branches
tuned the fast March air.
Flurries masked green buds.

How ironic now it seems,
the game played on vacations.
Hold your breath, you said,
until we pass the graveyard.
Face pressed against your legs
and carpet, sometimes I cheated.

Finally, you cheated me.

8

Nights I used to wonder
if the dead, planted, made the earth
wrinkle and slide like the sea,
or like those fields of granite
—wind wave and rock wave—cut by glacier.

Now I think of your forehead
no longer wrinkled, having let go
of all emotion.

9

March, sodden, bled away to April.
On my birthday I had a dream.

A tooth had loosened
to a taste like iron.

With two fingers I gripped the crown
and pulled it out.
No blood, but tiny sepals,
faint green leaves
that slowly blossomed in the sun
awakening me

to one last snow,
its glare in sunlight
harsh, a kind of trial.

April Fire

1

What is it we desire in spring,
or are we merely a part of desiring?
In early morning, birdsong trills
like running water. Something in us grows
from darkness.

Below these trees,
huge fountains that stand,
already the worms begin to slide
their alphabet

over white roots, white tendrils
that slowly unfurl, grow, and divide
finer than a woman's hair,

while the orange of robins
moves like flame across the lawn.

2

Finally the snow is gone,
I walk toward the pond.
See, the night's little gown
of mist still lingers; cold
air condensed to water, now
drawn off by hot April sun.

The first butterfly floats up.
Last fall, a legged worm,
it crawled onto a limb
and spun a cocoon. Some dissolve
to a formless jell, wintery-cold,
that will recombine, form
the brilliant wings and body.

Look, without a trace, the slow
tusk of ice has disappeared
with the thinning gown of mist.

As a child I used to think
all solid things were dead,
liquids alive, and that vapors
hovered above like the soul.

3

Each year I have watched the ritual.
Your pale hands and long white fingers
probing the earth,
searching out the bulbs and tubers
of daffodils and begonias
always in evening,

                              so as not
to shock them with light.

The pale shoots and growth buds of eyes
that you separate
with fingers like a surgeon's
then replant to form new life.

Even the rootstock of iris
I have seen you carefully divide.
Later in May, head bowed, I stood amazed,
dizzy among their lavender flags—

ranks of them, perfumed fences
bordering the farm.

Is it desire
having sprung from memory
that produces such lavish forms?

4

Spade over my shoulder
I stand in the three o'clock light.

Heel up, I shove the blade
into the earth, force

the handle down, then listen
for the hollow-chested rip.
Grass and weed root snap
as the sod begins to split.

On and on until six o'clock;
jigsawed and broken
the earth breathes new light.

Pocked like the topped-over soil
a half-moon floats above
while in the house your white head dozes
composing an evening dream.

Now I take seeds from my palm
one by one, poke them down
and draw the earth's thick blanket up
the way a mother tucks in a son

to sleep.
Above, in new dark, the moon
floats like a swollen spider
through the vast larvae of stars.

5

Now from the vertical
come the spiral works of spring.
For one month I have watched the thick tulip stalk grow
from a stout white thumb
breaking soil, unraveling green, to one
broad chamois leaf, then two
as the stem tapers

to a swollen lip,
its tall ovalish green
tinted to a purplish want.

How the sepals become finer, finer,
silken gauze to gossamer
like an insect's wings,

curtains that slowly open
toward the inner body
that shocks you with
the brilliant red
and sweetly vulgar tongue.

Have you not
waited with the bee
for the veils to unfold
and reveal rigid stamens
crowned by the anthers' fiery pollen,
talc-yellow-gold blowing
                              drifting deep
within the flower's fully blossomed cup?

6

Everywhere there is birth.
Like a broken piece of shadow
a spider scurries over dry earth
then clambers onto its web
filled with miniature offspring,
planets orbiting their sun.

A tiny beetle
lands on my chest.
His moist sticky shell
shines like a tree's new bud.
His hair-thin antennae shiver
crimson, measuring new space at last.

Doves collect in the pines.
A soft popping explodes
as a pair hovers up. Their wings
double   flutter   cross
and steady the air to conceive.

In the hot three o'clock sun
a Black Swallowtail lands
slowly fanning its wings
that stop in a trembling pause.

Tiny yellow swirls
suffused with dusty purple
kaleidoscope within my eyes
until I'm drunk with color.

But I go on staring deeper
to the absence of all color,
close my eyes, yet
stare deep enough to see
memory fade to intuition,

an opaque rose glow
through skin, blood's memory?

7

Now when the moon is dark
we plant those things
that grow beneath earth.
Darkness feeds dark
as light increases light
until from dark
a darker light begins to grow.

From a wicker basket I take
dried rootstock of carrot and beet,
poke them half-a-finger deep.

In two months' time
the spiked orange teeth
will range like fire upside down
among oval, purplish-red clouds.

You insist it's not too late
to plant the seed
potatoes.

Once in this same field
a neighbor girl dug one up.
She sat in the rough
sunlit earth. Long blond strands of hair

fell across her cheeks, rose
smeared with dirt.

Poor treasure, we washed
then split it with my knife to find
the clean stench of stone.

How mealy it tasted. How bland.
How dumb the little tombs of potatoes,
yet how simply, with plain white flowers
they resurrect themselves.

8

Still I can't forget
how the red-tailed hawk swept down
and lifted the wobbly pigeon up
high to an oak.

There with steel talons
he gripped it hard
and with hooked beak
stripped feathers from its wing.

Then, red bands of meat
he ripped from its breast
as the feathers sifted down
like a dogwood's blowing petals.

Later, I passed that spot
where the small, balding thing lay,
eyes rotting out
in the last bronze light.

What
nervous gold bloomed among feathers?
I saw them
crawl, dance, and tap.
Bees enameling the black.

Walking the slow way home
I stared at the sky's pale dome
until I saw talons of stars.

High in the south
between Leo and the Small Dog
the Crab's diamonded legs flared.
I stared like a small boy
trying to remember what a grownup said.

At the Crab's very center
lay the spiraled cluster *Praesepe*
once called *The Gate of Men.*
From its hive eternal souls
descended to those just born.

9

Tomorrow will be May.
I have risen early on
the eve of my mother's birthday.

I listen until I hear
silence inscribed in the song
of birds.

Slowly I will learn their language,
the transparent language of water.

All month
from the first seed sparks
April's slow green fire has burned.

Now the small gestures of plants
usher the summer in.

What we say on this earth
are words, light blooming

as though all our lives
were the slow unnaming of fire and water,
a movement from past to future.

And what is the future
but a memory perfect, without joy or regret
for those not here to remember.

The future is what the dead know
and by remembering
make it present yet.

July Stasis

1

Everything that rises
must by necessity come to a summit,
and thus for a moment, the rising
is supported by the downward movement.
Desire that we felt in spring
now balanced by an indifference in summer.
In nature this is a natural process
yet among humans it is tragic.

If desire is a liquid thing,
then I have felt innocence evaporate.
As a boy
I was led by my father through
a garden exotic and rare.

There for the first time
he pronounced the word *orchid*.

The petals, olive-green-maroon,
rakishly hued
with purple, enclosed a bone-white and brown-
speckled throat, from which stamens
like gluey prongs grew.

How I first turned away from the vulgar
only to be stricken by beauty.
There, working as in dream's
slow motion spaces,
two staggering bees held

like the sailors I had met in Köln,
their arms splayed out,
their necks collapsed
over opium.

It was there long ago
with my father in a garden
among drenched slow trickling sounds
that I stared at a fountain
and learned how rising water
is supported by water falling.

2

For two weeks I hoped
the clematis would bloom.
The pale two inch neck
leafless; yet hope
lies at the root
not in the stem.

Now
the small joy
of an old friend
equaled by two petals
unraveling.

What do the old hope for?
I stare at the rose
climbing the apricot tree.
Among the fruits' small cleft cheeks
the lavish bloom
of red.

3

July, the month not long begun,
and everything approaches a stellar calm.
By night, high in the sky's black dome
Cygnus plunges south
through the Milky Way's long cloud.

Now the brightest stars
of the Eagle, Swan, and Lyre
compose an equilateral triangle
that slides away with the oncoming fall.

If you stay up late
you will see threaded meteors hang,
cluster, pop, and break
like mulberries on a hot summer's day.

And if you stay up till dawn
you will no longer hear
the impetuous spring songs of birds,
for they have raised or lost their young.

And if you look about your garage
you will see spider webs
spun fine, dangling in the humid air
the way the Milky Way dangles higher.

And if you look closer
you will see, as if spinning there
about the fat, female spider
her tiny young circling like planets
thrown out by the conflagration of a star.

And if you walk out onto your lawn
you will see the roses'
spiraled petals blossomed out full
as if to accept some thing from above,

something weighted, cumbrous, and about to fall.
And if you keep walking, there is no end
for you have entered
the middle of all things.

4

                    Our cottage lies on the lake.
From green swale, waves crest cottony-white
then smash against the pier's great rocks
spouting water up
that more illumined climbs.

I stare back at the beach.
Youthful radios blare
among bikinis fleshed bright by sun
while the laughter of children rises
from wave and sand.

Here, the summer
following my mother's death
I half-unwilling flirted with a woman,
kissed her in the diamond glare
then caressed her in the shade.

Beneath the white glare of a neighbor's awning,
a hornet's gun-blue abdomen hangs,
slowly bobbing in air. While just below
like clustered rubies
raspberries sag among thorns.

5

Fire on water is a great scale
of balance. The sun falls
over the earth's slow curve
the way the mind on sleep's horizon
sifts gently toward dark.

Across the lake, the red sun
scuttles sideways like a crab.
Flakes of orange
dissolve to burnt umber.

Now I know why
we tend to think of love in evening,
as though its own clear light
might extend the day.

6

Showers of diamonds, rubies, shattered emeralds,
the slowly paced colors of a roman candle,
their pause and held breath of thunder
remembered now like a wealthy hangover.

I watch them burst from tiny pods,
the hubs of lavish spirals.
Enormous berries, ripened bursts
of fuchsia, magenta, and plum hang clustered,

prefaced by brief flowers of smoke
that often outlive the fruit.

Like all things that flower
they branch, curve, and spiral out—
all that was vertical now exchanged
for the lavish and decadent.

There, like a thousand pounds of gold
hammered powder thin, goes
a giant pinwheel. Two spiraling arms
swoosh, smearing lavish dust across the black,
until flattened like an egg
resemble the Milky Way.

As a child, I remember watching on TV
the first space launches at Cape Canaveral.
There, on our bouncing screen, because the camera
could not track such vertical speed,
the finned rocket moved

ejecting each of its jet-propelled stages
until it broke gravity's arms
in a miraculous slow arcing curve.
Only once was I

as sad. I had read
somewhere about the death of stars,
how it often takes hundreds of years
before we see their lights expire.

7

                    Memory distills
a kind of joy, makes the general
specific, until all we see
are a bridge's rafters, a boy and man
glimpsed through leaves
above the bearded rush of stream
hushed, and always sunlit in the mind.

                    Here my first vivid memory
remains intact. The trout
I threaded from the glassy falls. You laughed
with joy at my first catch
as I danced back
startled by its flopping on the bridge.

Now I am startled again
by what remains the same. Everything
unchanged because it moves
somewhat in ratio?
                    You say that maple
is twenty feet higher. Sumac grown wild
all over, while I feel like a child
simply because I haven't noticed
anything, except that the stream is low,
the bridge's steel
rafters green.

Now with a kind of patience
we walk the stream bed
dry, where water, once veined
with silver fishes, flowed.

Huge rocks whose tops
we knew as crested falls
are now exposed,
a fish's skeleton enlarged,

and we, stepping over
the bleached white bones, are
changed by place, forced to remember
what we never saw

until the dark, imaginary map
is rooted in the brain,
never pulled loose till now.

8

Toward the month's end, and everything has begun
to fall. The trees, for a season
deepening in color, now begin to pale.
August, one says the word exhaling.

The days, with their attic-trapped breath,
sag. Lettuce wilts in the ninety-degree sun
that swelters through haze. Inside,
notes stuck to the wall with tape
loosen and remain half-hung.

Outside, along the gravel-tar road,
pokeweed and wild carrot bathe in the dust
raised by an occasional pickup truck.
Then, indistinguishable as it is far off,

a muffled rumble. Did the half-built frame
of a house collapse? Leaves, silverish-
hued, shiver against
the violet expanse of blue.

> *Four months before my mother died*
> *she accidently broke a crystal vase.*
> *So finely had it shattered, my father says*
> *he still finds splinters lodged*
> *in cracks of the pine-slat floor,*
> *or hidden in the nap of our Chinese rug.*

     Steam rose
from the tarred road
as I walked down our drive
and stared at the dripping trees to hear
birdsong evaporate in sun.

    The cottonwood
its trunk ragged with fungus
had lost a limb, and the humid air
smelled of sawed wood. Southeast and higher
like faded pastels in a Chinese silk

a rainbow spanned the sky. Saddened, I stared
at the beautiful lie,
its prismed intricacy. Is it the green
which separates violet from red?

That night I dream
that together we are walking down
a twilit bed of stones.
But when I ask you why
there is no water, you turn words
like braille

—Don't ask but follow—
east to where the tea-colored light
turns dawn-yellow. There
you draw slowly from your hip
a knife for fileting fish

and in dream's unastonished tenor
cut with ease
into a boulder,
remove a slice like melon
which you hand to me

at the precise moment I scream
not at the acrid, mealy taste
of nothing

but at your gaping, toothless smile.

9

The last sultry day of July
my father waves from the porch.
Along the fence, nightshade climbs tall.

From out of the mouths of violet blossoms
bright green berries push
toward red.

In one of evening's final glades
I watch tiny insects jig
translucent paths
with wings that cast

a faint transparent hue
celebrating that moment when
light flares like a grandiloquent fountain
before falling to its basin.

I watch until the blue horizon falls
upon our green small-bellied hills
where, like bubbles of champagne rising,
lights of fireflies slowly dissolve.

October Stars

1

What April gave,
each greening place
a renaissance of fringed detail,
slowly undone in autumn,

gives back time's
echo. The thinning crowns of trees
perform a solitary act
approaching song.

The light that had begun to shift in August
now seems consummate
in decline. Each day the sun
slips further toward the south, its metaled way
pale as the desiccate pulp of an orange.

In afternoon the fields are a gathering
of fecund smells. Overripened and dry
they brandish a blond light
teeming with the rise and fall
of cicada hum.

The dry hills are scarved with goldenrod
so thick at times, its slow swale
shines like a lake
from which yellow streams flow
toward roadside and ditchbank,

a lesser shore where one finds
like exotic shells, or starfish,
the blue-fringed chicory
and Queen Anne's Lace.

Ricocheting about the pond
a medley of frog twang
slowly thins as I approach
stepping around skeined webs of silk
and tentpoles of grass, elegantly
jeweled with snakespit.

Bleached emerald and spatulate still
as a lotus leaf
the pond's moss-bottomed mirror reflects
slow-blossoming clouds
marred only by the waterstriders,
whose glide heals invisibly
with each fine-haired stroke.

Beyond like a larger pond
our garden reels with life.
The yarrow now four feet high
holds up on stems a sulphurous coral
where butterflies like blown petals flit.

Acorn squash and pumpkins squat
—ochre, yellow, and orange—
swollen to ridiculous shapes
attached to thin, fuselike vines.

Toward what end do they burn
while bees drowse in the phlox?

2

This anticipation before frost,
like the hunter's great loneliness
till he finds the beast?
The deer, its tawny sunlit panels
drift in and out of shade.

And the way he aims—
like that animal's gaze
filling the dusk,

and the one shot
a perfect moon
on its sky?

How tall we stood
over the dead body

as the slow speech
of our breathing rose
to the yellow tent of maples.

Half way home
the sun's pale yolk
broke through rows of purple cloud,
cast gold on scarlet trees
and flooded the inside of our car.

Like a boy in church
I watched all this
through the dried blood
on the windshield.

3

Everywhere yellow prevails.
Stems of goldenrod, ragwort, and fennel
swell with odd-shaped cocoons,
while beyond these sulphurous shades
wait the stubborn truths of brown.

At wood's edge blushing scarlet
among a line of yellow maples,
the pronged red fruit of the sumac
poise, brilliant as cardinals.

Evening's watercolor clouds
move closer to earth
while across the meadow's brow
chiseling shadows like cold blades inch
drawing from the ground
a richer weed-tanged scent.

All that was spring's,
a crescendo of daybreak music,
now recurs at dusk.
Sparrows thick as locusts
chatter in the tops of trees
hung with a copperish-gold light.

The once sharp cicada pitch
has fallen to a slur. These cooler nights
depend on a music
where insects shy beneath rocks.

High overhead, though still faint,
the Swan begins to shine
as she climbs toward her death.
The solemn dark is ushered in

by a solo cricket's speech.

4

Speech of fire, speech of water, and speech of the geese
departing. We stand in the paper fruit of leaves
raking, strumming them into a long pile
down which the orange flames scale,
roving tongues that lisp
naming everything
once.

The sun casts a pale emerald stroke
tinting gold through the pines.
Wood smoke lies thick in the crystal air

        and all is still
except the rhythmic echo
of an axe.

Now I place stones in the fire,
and dream of winter trees.
How memory undermines desire.

        In the dream the screen door opens.
        Mother is there. She calls me in for dinner.
        I hum all the way across the lawn.
        Everything is just the same
        except the sun no longer falls across the window
        but shines with a stationary glow,
        and though we go on eating
        there is no longer any desire to move.

5

                    you
tumbling down   from your chair
heart flutter   and fail
constriction   of arteries
the muffled pop   in your chest
a mess I can't   see

but imagine   the cardinal
black-masked   fluttering up
to catch a bee   in flight
red feathers   spattering green

6

Death comes like a fine trip abroad
in which some things are always left
undone, the letter to a friend, and bill
unpaid, but all the what-ifs come about.

How weak your script had become,
the once sharp serifs and rounded curves.
Had someone slowly tightened
the string of years running through your words?

In a bottom dresser drawer,
games which we had played,
and an ivory-colored skeleton.
How the skull grows from the spine
the way a flower blossoms from its stem.

7

Now like a chorus of shadows
led by the black-robed pastor
our dark suits surround the casket.

Now like the solemn current
of a river moving toward the sea
our broken voices murmur the Lord's Prayer.

Now looking up among the shattered glances
I can almost read location
in the creased lines of faces.

8

After everyone left, I came back.
I hated the bouquets,
the junkpile of flowers.

But already
a squirrel ran
the pile of rubble for a nut,

late bees prowled the stamens of flowers —
and the body,
the body in the ground
like a sugar cube in water
began its slow dissolve.

The rain, sunlit, carried the opulence of fire,
and as the sky slowly cleared
a small plane sputtered, and began again.

9

In the pale liquid evening sky
blue gradually distills
to deeper blue.

I walk out along the pier
and sit beneath a blond willow's limbs
that rise and fall in a mild southwest wind.

Low in the east,
sallow-white and pale, the moon's
chalked vowel of wonder
balances the sun,

and I feel my heart like a small planet
swing between the two.

Holding onto the willow
I lean toward my buoyant face
until I can almost hear among waves
the rapt silence of the dead.

Above, sugary
and far the first stars
hang near-fruit among leaves.

And there, like smoke closing
the twilit air, a last hatch of insects
rises to die.

        Stars,
galaxies, too, have their seasons.
And when the planets spin
in their slow ellipses
I wonder what thin harmonies they make.

About the Author

As a boy, Mark Irwin lived near the national Nuclear Research Laboratory in Oak Ridge, Tennessee, where the blue glow he observed from the laboratory's "high-flux swimming pool reactor"—used to isolate neutrons, then "fired" to split atoms—made an indelible impression on his mind and, later, on his poetry. Born in Faribault, Minnesota, Irwin was graduated from Case Western Reserve University (B.A. 1974, Ph.D. 1982) and the University of Iowa (M.F.A. 1980).

An associate professor of literature and philosophy at the Cleveland Institute of Art, Irwin has also taught at Case Western Reserve University and the University of Akron. In 1981 he was a Fulbright fellow to Romania. He received a Discovery/*The Nation* award in 1984 and an Ohio Arts Council Fellowship in 1986. He is the author of *The Halo of Desire*, and the translator of *Notebook of Shadows*, by Philippe Denis, and *Ask the Circle to Forgive You: Selected Poems of Nichita Stănescu, 1964–1979*.

About the Book

Against the Meanwhile was composed on a Compugraphic MCS 100 Digital Typesetting System in Trump Mediaeval, a contemporary typeface based on classical prototypes. Trump Mediaeval was designed by the German graphic artist and type designer Georg Trump (1895–1986). It was initially issued in 1954, by C.E. Weber Typefoundry of Stuttgart, in the form of foundry type and linecasting matrices. *Against the Meanwhile* was composed by Lithocraft of Grundy Center, Iowa; designed and produced by Kachergis Book Design of Pittsboro, North Carolina.

WESLEYAN UNIVERSITY PRESS, 1988